Hundred-Mile Home

Hundred-Mile Home

A Story Map of Albany, Troy, & the Hudson River

Susan Petrie

Foreword by
Mark Wunderlich

excelsior editions

AN IMPRINT OF STATE UNIVERSITY OF NEW YORK PRESS

Cover photo of the Hudson River by Susan Petrie. Design by
Lisa N. Comstock

Photos and sketches by Susan Petrie

Page 45, fragment of painting, "Curiosity of the Magua" by Len Tantilllo.
Used with permission.

Page 52, ink drawing by Ana Novaes (Insta: Itg.art)

Previously published poems:
"to 5W" terrain.org (2019)
"Early Evening on 4th Street," "A History of Disappearance," "Lock," and
"Grain," Bloodroot Literary Journal (2017)

Published by State University of New York Press, Albany

© 2021 Susan Petrie

Excelsior Editions is an imprint of State University of New York Press

For information, contact State University of New York Press, Albany, NY
www.sunypress.edu

Library of Congress Cataloging-in-Publication Data

Name: Petrie, Susan, author.
Title: Hundred-mile home: a story map of Albany, Troy, & the
    Hudson River / Susan Petrie.
Description: Albany : State University of New York Press, [2021].
Identifiers: ISBN 9781438483009 (pbk. : alk. paper) | ISBN
    9781438482996 (ebook)
Further information is available at the Library of Congress.

10 9 8 7 6 5 4 3 2 1

"Poetry is less a genre than it is a way of being and seeing."
C. D. Wright

"Once a landscape goes undescribed and therefore unregarded it becomes more vulnerable."
Barry Lopez

"Expose yourself to places no one goes."
W. G. Sebald

"For the Apache imagination, geography and history are consubstantial. Placeless events are inconceivable."
Keith Basso

Foreword

Seventeen years ago, I moved into a haunted house. It was a modest stone structure built nearly 300 years earlier in Greene County, New York, on the western side of the Hudson River and close to a narrow watercourse called Corlaer's Creek. The creek, with its steep drop-off that ends at the river, has its source somewhere above the unincorporated hamlet of Hamburg and marks the border between the townships of Catskill and Athens.

The house, I would learn, was built by a Dutch family on the occasion of the marriage of a daughter. Like many historic structures scattered about the mid-Hudson region, it had fallen into ruin: pipes had frozen and burst; a hole in the roof let in rain and weather; squirrels, raccoons, bats, and snakes (!!) had moved in; the yard was a thicket of trash, brush, weed trees, and poison ivy.

Anyone who saw the house told me not to buy it. But, newly arrived from Cape Cod with little knowledge of the area and well-meaning notions of restoration and renewal, I bought it anyway. I had felt something toward the house—a connection suggestive of a rich but opaque history.

As I began the long process of renovation and restoration, this work revealed an enduring vernacular genius held by the house's builders and previous occupants. The house was surprisingly plumb, the stained-glass windows built some time in the 1950's were both extravagant and cheerful, the angles and rooms well-proportioned.

This house, set in the lee of a hill, has been a kind of set for an historical drama whose full text is lost. As ownership has shifted over the course of generations, moving back and forth between restoration and neglect, I see myself as part of its history. I know too that my hold is temporary and that it will outlive me—if houses do in fact "live"—as it had outlived all of its previous occupants. That knowledge, though, has not prevented me from the daunting work of recovery.

The work of affectionate recovery bestowed upon the structures we call home may also be extended to a landscape, a region, a place, as illustrated by Susan Petrie in *Hundred-Mile Home: A Story Map of Albany, Troy, & the Hudson River*. She felt a similar connection suggestive of a rich but opaque history which she has given her time and labor to uncover and clear away. As homeowners, we succumbed to a very human need to explore and discover, to imagine and decipher codes inherent in craftsmanship, to find and piece together a story in what remains, to build and rebuild connection.

∼

In *Hundred-Mile Home*, Petrie has chosen to slow down and linger in these forgotten places, to conduct a kind of poetic archeology of place, an uncovering and reimagining of the filament that still connects Albany, Troy, and a section of the Hudson River through the geography and typography, architecture, and people who have lived and died in this once-important region. While her book records a lived experience, it is also a sort of ghost story, a lyric sequence that awakens the reader to a hidden history in which both living and dead are rediscovered and allowed a chance to speak.

For years now, Petrie has driven the back roads of the mid- and upper-Hudson, walked and hiked its streets and trails, photographed its collapsing barns and burned mills, drawn out the poetry of graffiti and forgotten signs. She is an explorer with an elegiac sensibility, and as she moves through the pessimism of post-industrial, post agricultural landscapes and rubble, she locates and pieces together the remnants of what was once a more hopeful past. In the act of piecing together, Petrie finds a deep connection to place where others may have seen very little.

It is important to note that *Hundred-Mile Home* is not a nostalgic book. As much as Petrie seems to argue on behalf of a thoughtful preservation of architecture and landscape, she explores the places of neglect and ruin with an eye for unexpected poignancy. Sometimes it is the ruination and decrepitude that draws her in for a closer look, other times it is the unspoken power of what is revealed at low tide.

Petrie is also an accomplished photographer, and the images interspersed throughout this book take a variety of forms—sometimes befogged and romantic, sometimes as documents of decay—though my favorites capture attempts to memorialize and instruct. Her inclusion of tilting blue historical markers show how, when devoid of context, even these attempts at permanence can become mysterious and disconnected from the story they hoped to memorialize. Like these blue plaques, Petrie's poems and lyrical fragments are signposts on a landscape whose inhabitants participated in an early idea of America, but that have—for myriad reasons—gone quiet.

∽

Not long after I started to renovate and restore my house, I began to meet the neighbors whose curiosity compelled them to drive into my yard to have a proper snoop. On three occasions, strangers told me that my house was haunted, suggesting that, as an outsider, the history of this house and this place was not something that I could own or perhaps even understand. I was seen as an interloper whose presence indicated yet another wave of regional opportunism. What neither of us knew was that I have my own Hudson Valley ghosts—a fifth great grandfather from a colonial Dutch family who drowned in the Schoharie Creek one freezing winter night on his way home from Albany when his sledge was thrown off a collapsing bridge. Buried in Glen, New York, under a stone that tells the story of his tragic death, this blood history was unknown to me until very recently. My own dead are buried here too, though for the seventeen years I have lived in the region, I had no idea of the connection.

I hope you will find in *Hundred-Mile Home* a necessary and lyrical invitation to connect, to remember, and to welcome the spirit of home back into view.

Mark Wunderlich

Introduction

In the spring of 1689, Bashō surrendered to a compulsion and set out on foot to explore the interior landscape of Japan. Over the course of many miles he recorded his encounters with sages and townspeople, and made subtle observations on mountains bathed in moonlight, delicate flowers and birds, temples, and historic ruins, many mossed over and forgotten. When he returned, he gathered his contemplations into a prose-poem diary, *Narrow Road to the Great North*, which was published posthumously. *Narrow Road* not only recorded his thoughts but served as a record to "re-story" places and events no longer appreciated or understood.

In 2015, Robert Macfarlane's *Landmarks* was published. Similarly, Macfarlane, a U.K.-based writer, took to his landscape and library and gathered up a massive glossary of terrain, to give us back the words to describe the visual bounty offered by woods and waters, mountains and trees, holloways and underlands. In one of my favorite chapters, "Bastard Countryside," he discusses how it took years to learn to write about his home, a place he describes as the jittery ground between city and country, "the edgelands." Victor Hugo called these places "bastard countryside," while others used names like "soft estate," "messy limbo," "guerilla ecology," and "transit zone." These are the places between city and country where history, nature—along with the stuff no one seems to care about anymore—gets pushed. Wetlands and water-falls, crows and gulls, boxcars and barges, bricks from demolished buildings, tributaries and train tracks to nowhere. These places with no names teem with curiosities that most people speed past on the way to somewhere else.

As a Troy native who had one of those wonderful, free-ranging childhoods, I was exploring edgelands when I was 10 years old. I still remember what it felt like to stumble upon Mount Ida Falls one winter morning, wandering about the urban/rurals of Hillsview Heights. Standing there alone and in awe, I wondered, *Do the grown-ups not know?* as water gushed through a hole in a massive wall of ice, the traffic of Spring Avenue 100 yards away.

Several years ago, I started to earnestly explore the cities, countryside, and edgelands in and around Albany, Troy, and the Hudson River, down the dirt roads and into the places visited by fishermen, the occasional hiker, and various individuals who seemed forgotten by time. Discovering the remains of what felt like the region's former magnificence has been a joy; I was able to roam and forage like a child, asking, "What's this?" and "How did this get here?" There is still evidence of a place that once pulsed with activity, industry, and people who did incredible things. Many of those people and events, however, have been forgotten and become irrelevant. The thread of our narrative has been broken.

America as an idea is a little over 400 years old, still very young. Upstate New York, specifically this mid-Hudson region where the Mohawk and Hudson converge, is a world-class landscape that hides in plain sight, framed by mountains to the north and south, with magnificent rivers and many wild pockets. It is a place where some of the nation's early capitalism took root and flourished, where the drama of trade and trapping, indentured workers and feudal landowners, discovery and creativity, exploitation and predatory maneuvers worked themselves out, shaping some of the best and worst characteristics of the country. If people were generally familiar with its history . . . Dutch, English, industrial, transportation . . . pride and shame would certainly co-mingle. Yet, with demolition and without context, many legends have been lost, and much of what has survived is neglected, unnamed, misunderstood, and relegated to the edgelands. The fate that has befallen this region is shared by numerous cities, towns, and villages across America. It's been inspiring to watch how the COVID-19 pandemic has helped people—now closer to home—reconnect to their regions. I'm hopeful that story maps will enter our literary lexicon and become a useful and necessary genre.

Hundred-Mile Home is just one version of discovery. I tried to get into as many backyards as I could, and I know I have missed some. That's why I think it's important for people to have some curiosity, to go out and learn for themselves about what was here, to seek and report back before it's gone entirely. There are still faint lines—and some stubborn brick and iron—that, with a little imagination, can reconnect us to our story.

SP
2020

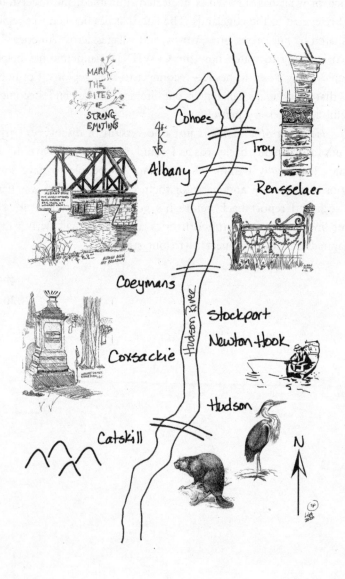

Hundred-Mile Home

Here, a democratic tide. What comes in must go, steady rhythm of disappearance. Wash of memory known to throw its shoulder against the living, counterweight of longing, curved & centuries deep, the big unseen. Here, the possibility of entering the cross-haze of remembrance, arousing forgottens, smeared with past of every skin, to seek those who eventually dropped tooth & bent down to the river to die. Or

resisted & lived out their silent second lives, hugging shore as refusing to give up this place just yet. Held wordlessly among us. Rises river, falls river, shows and hides its ruined piers & piling fields, what was done then dumped, stashed, traded off, shot, whacked, smoked, chipped, wore down further, blown to dust, scattered around inside this dirty earth & left unnamed. Then, in the elegance of invisible forgotten, a calamity of green growing up & over. Outlines, footfalls, disparaged or heaved or flattened or downed beneath a paveway. Here, is where I find myself: outside the wall of memory. Though willing. Finding their road, their ferry, their post, their nail rot, their flint & gun of place, their fish beaver bark chimney bridge brick sail steam train flight electric slip . . .

Then mark the weeds, for they have done their work.

H O M E

this place of endurance . . . plain residence or
domicile . . . one's hardy social unit . . . to forge by
living together . . . a familiar . . . to have one's domestic
attention . . . could be a place of origin . . . could mark by
establishment (rumored to provide care for people
with special need) . . . place of return, perennially . . . thus
relating to any man/woman/child/animal/beloved
when returning by instinct to its territory after
leaving . . . move or be aimed toward with accuracy . . .
one's land or living quarters, or simply, a place where
one likes to be . . . restful or congenial place . . . where
something flourishes, under freedom from attack . . .
ménage . . . a headquarters . . . this native habitat . . . to the
center or heart of deeply . . . any place of refuge . . . to be
guided to a destination by signals . . . hearth, fireside,
asylum, shelter, bungalow, cottage, chalet, bunkhouse,
condominium, chateau, billet, dorm, duplex, of a
palace, of a tabernacle & of the human body as the
abode of demons that possess it . . .

Origins: Germanic, Old English: hām
Dutch: heem, huis, vaderland
Mahican: Pempotawuthut—the praying place, or place of the council fire at
Albany, New York.
Sacred ground beneath I-787. This corporation, this trading post.

I was striding over the distant past & waiting
for you in a map of dreams

To be held tight by Troy, by Albany is: to
be in this place of so profound a familiarity
as to be unnoticed. To be of this [capitol]
region, unstoried upper Hudson, occupying
a convergence of waters, riot of invisible
lore, plus those who birthed each lucid
& anonymous inventor, each maker, each
digger, doer & finder of raw. Almost gone
dark beneath the thatch of time. Hold tight:
I am imagining you back . . .

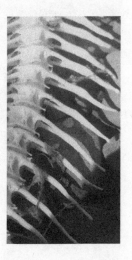

(recall: there were no pilgrims here)
$$$
Hundred-mile home

Repatriation

Days pass, I continue to approach. It never occurs to me the more I am walking toward home the further away it becomes. Day after day, buildings are receding, the river is receding. Finally, my brothers become impatient and they are receding.

Sun raking itself across my face. Compass melting. Horizon lifting herself, is heaving herself across the sky, reminding me this is what happens when night forgets to show up.

Landscape keeps rolling past. In someone else's imagination, the air is thickening, seeding clouds. Mist is beginning as children are falling away, forgetting to return. Sound of the cardiac perimeter dilating.

I am here now, but I am resisting.

> *wants to return*
> *youth to*
> *her wordless place*

A Place Is Named for Good Deeds

Pheasant feather, mitten:
she descends

Until thirty, what she'd known at nine
remained unclear

Then found it named: Mount Ida
Falls, at nine

Worked her way inside
its gush & frozen waterfall

startled spray, rivulets
of plumes & mists

Youth-girl believes in
the crossing of streets,

her
narrow paths of want

Learns curiosity rewards,
so does she descend into a place within

Door creaks   shadow lengthens   comes the melting rain.

> *Where on summer nights*
> *& the sound a train puts*
> *through her now*

Mount Ida Falls, Poestenkill Gorge, tributary. The firemen know how many
locals jump in/ fall in/ drop in from wherever. Why barriers in Troy burn.
Far back, a paper mill. Then iron. Now shards, railroad spikes, mill wheel,
stairs with missing steps, drainpipe, spring thaw. Once, a watering fall.

So pass the match

pass the hatchet,

the wirecutters, too

Topophilia: I

Terrain: mythical familiar, mythical unfamiliar. Encroaches at a young age. Buzzes about the back door. Holds youth in concentricity. Not quite east side, raised ranches cluster, project cluster, ring of wildness, unnamed trees & weeds, by woods, by surface streets, ovaloid curbs, enclave for raising kids. But a neighborhood, all that's written within it, all that touches it, makes it fluid, unknown.

Then that day she goes unwalled. Lifts chain link metal latch & backyard freedom flees anointing youth. The body smelling its own escape, sites, marks, maps, runs on fours, touches, digs, balances unfamiliar, tests weights & tethers. Eyes transcribe. Eyes pocket. Eyes build navigation. Landmarks. Declination of sound, of touch. Which way that corner leads to tree to garden to cliff to pond through swaths of ferns down paths, ravines, cross bridge.

Adults: barely remember the freedoming of their selves. One winter girl walks, the zwer of pheasants exploding from brush. Declination. Rasp of hawk on barren field. Declination. Orients. Just Roaming. Passing to summer, same field known by its sweltering burr of crickets + hot breath of every kind of weed + the secretions of spit bugs.

Moves beyond rings of safety to an entire day made of clay, and by August, densely cool to touch. Her body, alone, curious, now inscribed. Her home the unwalled outside. Animates everyone's ignored. Sees the unseen. Handles the forgotten.

By her feet is how she knows.

h e e m

A researcher, once, with confidence said

["] . . . *in the West we may feel sentimental or nostalgic attachment to the places we've lived, but in the end we see them as separate from our inner selves.*["]

Topophilia: II

Dip.
      Condom wrappers. Beer
cans.

Take the backstair down to youth: Mount Ida Falls. Most have no idea. Save the lovers and the vandals, counted among us, the curious, we arrive at odd hours—midnight, dawn. If you've been here, leave something:

      Floating diner menu. Scorched
         timber. Glass butt plug. One
      black sock.

Fledglings fledge. Froth froths. Widths to cross, stone to stone, ascending shale, water pounds. Ten minutes in the distance arms arise, two men filthy & clinging in a bus shelter sleep & waterfront yoga carries on.

      I love warm ketchup
         + the charred wooden
      safety bar

She asks the terrain: what if: "No Trespassing" transforms to graded steps / What if: history's sterilization commission arrives. Erects durable plastic sepia photoshows. The familiar frowning working poor. Sepia explains Iron. Sepia explains Smelting. Sepia explains Child Labor & What They Administered to Mules.

What if: grass planted / What if: wheelchair access

First, she complained no one cared
Then feared they would
         She'll want her vandals back

Burden Iron Works
History of Disappearance

It's called the understory
    It's what springs up from the forest floor

Springs up from the forest floor beneath trees
    Beneath trees but there's nothing here

Nothing here, except dry leaves
    Except dry leaves

And stacks of mossy iron ore, iron slag
    Slag and two rusty hand cranks
    Hand cranks

Can you feel how *heavy* this is?
    Imagine

Imagine one thousand Sons of Vulcan. In unison.
    90,000 tons of coal
    600 tons of horseshoes barreled in a week

The magnificence of their labor. The menace.
Their waterwheel. Sixty feet of spin, whir.
    Their Work.

Now, just tree trunks with a canopy
Not even branches, no
    Not branches, not even weeds.

Memory Toy

Like thousands of other things in the world, it [the waterwheel] has seen its day and has now nothing but a history. There are old timers in the southern section who regard it almost with veneration and can recall the time when it was the moving power that kept a great factory going and was looked upon as a remarkable institution. It is many a day since it made a revolution. Dilapidation o'erspreads it and it is gradually disintegrating.

Troy Press, August 10, 1903

Or:
Unfortunately, those in local government see these buildings as eyesores and not the potential tourism revenue generating resources they can become . . .

Or:
This complex, this rolling mill, owned by the city, has been allowed to rot and several of the buildings have collapsed.

Or:
Demolition by neglect.

Or:
The scrap man's ad on the city bus:
"Recycling our present to conserve our future."

Or:
What happened here.
What's our story. And why.

Slash Tender

Now the land is
becoming dull and slow,

& the river clouded, split apart, and dead
the ambitious are the first to go.

The factories are closing
their entire languages are dissolving

& the vigorous click of routines is ceasing
tools and machines are being weighed, flattened, sold for scrap,

buildings are being demolished,
or left to be obscured by time, by nature.

Then, our connection to both land and work is passing
our imaginations, no longer in tact,

& we are helping our children escape
quietly, we are strangling with gloved hands

the inheritance
of our private miseries.

---

*"The steel that made New York a city was wrought in my lifetime.
A town that crawled now stands erect. And we whose backs were bent
above the puddling hearths know how it got its spine."*
James J. Davies, *The Iron Puddler: My Life in the Rolling Mills*

Miserable Children in Historic Places

Because we're from here
it's a place
we really should consider leaving

"New York is a living vertical fiber in the development of the world." —*Harold W. Thompson*

Hard Sledding

Each urge to flee forges another chain in me
Frances Ponge

I've watched you bored, burning pallets
fishing when the weather turns

down streets no one really uses
breaking bottles by the river

drained of all desire to leave
Hudson Dusters

hey 518 Club—
having ugly fun, though I
            can't muster the speed

needed to pop wheelies
on the Menands Bridge.
            Much less drive away.

So even the shad are running.

So more children are born here
soft, then angled

enough to live down dreams
& eventually learning to spell

I've seen them playing
on the same dead streets of winter

no one really uses, with
coats unzipped & bootless

helping each other through
unplowed snow, climbing car roofs

sliding down windshields
no sleds & just for fun

Tough Love Ghazal

"There's a lot of potential down there in Troy."
That's what Lou Rosmilla says, the Mayor of Troy.

Homer's *Iliad* launched legends and heroes,
launched one thousand ships when Greece fought Troy.

Its demolition was cheered a few years back,
the USS Monitor's deck plates pressed in Troy.

Blue Dodge Dart, 3 kids stuck in back,
Crossing the Menands bridge, down toward Troy.

Painted *hydria*, vases black with gold
History vividly recorded, after the sack of Troy.

The God's weren't angry when our Iron Works burned,
once an industrial mecca, here in Troy.

Brenda Ann's photos flash open our streets, upstate
girls, tats, black with white cracks all over Troy.

John Emmett paints what he likes,
Sno-Cone, the Music Hall, dual emblems of Troy.

We ran Black Pipe, tunneled where we weren't seen
dumped us out past projects, on edges past Troy.

This city's motto: *Ilium fuit, Troja est*
so sue me. It's Troy.

> *"I am so glad not to live in that place.*
> *You know, the air, then that smell of the river water. Ugh."*
> *Woman from Vermont*

Early Evening on 4th Street

Behind the brick factory stack
already the moon is visible
a sheer papery disk.

The Frito-Lay truck
bounces from 4th to Canal
its axels

straddling holes
and patched pavements.

Boys on bikes
race the wrong way
down one-way streets,

while three fireman lounge
out front of the station
frowning,

tapping quiet codes
on their phones

as tiny petals draw down
from spring's flowering trees

collecting in lacy piles
on slate sidewalks,
on street corners,

and in the rusty
raised letters
of circular sewer caps

Heavy Duty Glossary of Enchantment

        lammies   *clinkers*

culm   *frog hack*   *shot blaster*

     pick clock   *battery hand*
bale breaker   *win the clay*
              bleach
       starch

puddle
   coil slit
   mold   *flying shearman*

dish the cinders   *tease the furnace*   *draw the*
   bloom from the squeezer

       jiggsie   *doffer*   *fixer*
   drawing-in girl   *cloth boy*
smash piecer

mule spindle   *ring spindle*

    jennie   *slash tender*   *steenbakker*
bobbin boy

  Jump Steady *spatting* *luting*

          wheeler setter
   sander
skull cracker craneman

        and namely plain

Shanty-Boy

Plate press
rebar car
spring iron pile
bring

on some
dead weight
tons. Or
move on.

Lest it rust-
by-the-mountain
by-the-acre

crescent of rust

crescent veined
his rust-lined
palm

Lest one
blue eye
its sclera

puckered
sets up with
his Irish by

the X
of railroad
to track
to weigh

to trade

to flatten,
fulsomely,
entirety of
a city's
underthings
. to China

We look at it like this: use it, then let it go. Industrial Revolution exploded then ended. Crush it. Sell it. Forget it. Be the practical one here and include everything we invented. Empire washes out. No evidence. We could remember the places of our successes and failures, but choose no.

A healing river.

a landscape's meaning will also be measured in loss

[dih-mol-ish] v.

1- to destroy or ruin (a building or other structure),
especially on purpose; tear down, raze
2 - to put an end to; destroy; explode
3 - to lay waste to; ruin utterly
4 - *informal.* to devour completely

---

from Middle French demoliss-

"*The air in New Netherland is as dry, pure, and wholesome as could be desired . . .*"
Adriaen van der Donck, 1655

Landmark H20vliet

One hundred and fifty years scatter down
        one-way streets. Neighbors divided

by boasts: *hallelujah*, or loudly, *knock*
        the damn thing down. A wound the size

of an April sky opens, thousands of bricks
        tumble, arches, a 3-story nave of ivory

filigree its Sunday ritual baptisms
        marriages. *But St. Patrick's, you're goin'*

down. For weeks, mist dampens
        demolition's constant and holy dust.

Easy to blame Dan's Hauling & Demo,
        men paid to aim the yellow claw skyward

toward the copper roof, where it nuzzles,
        sniffs, clenches, mechanically repeats. Easy,

too, to blame ourselves speechless over
        taxes . . . negligence . . . or better:

the grocery store chain wheedling for the space.
        Suddenly, landmark we once believed—

is mortal. Watervliet, leafless, longing,
        leaning city, too poor to afford its beauty.

Mary & Joseph boxed, crated, sold south.
    The gold cross dropped from your skyline

loosed from the tower, your Meneely bell.

---

1. *Landmark* (Old English): an object in the landscape, which by its conspicuousness, serves as a guide in the direction of one's course. What is the word for what happens within when one's landmark leaves. Or when destroyed on purpose by another.

2. Meneely bell manufacturers, established in 1826, set up in Watervliet (West Troy). Once exported around the country, the world. Once (I would imagine) a source of pride.

Not like the bombing of Dresden
no, not all at once
but the . . . attitude
working the streets:

    that vanishes buildings
    deletes
    evidence there was
    something shared or known

when the cared for
is disappearing
and those who know
silent, at lunch counters

"*I'm not nostalgic, but there are buildings you have to keep. They belong to the country's patrimony.*" *Elias Khoury*

Margaret, 1938
She has been swimming in the Erie Canal

As if once
there was a canal

a Lock 1
she swan-dived

into the place
where there was a canal

she touched
touched, face first

into the water, slurried water
from a river

her friends dove in
dove in too, into the canal

where there was once a canal
and an intake valve

it opened, the valve
as if Margaret was fourteen

into the Lock
diving, intake valve open, an arm

Bev's arm, locks around her neck
Margaret's neck, saving her, the arm

when the intake valve opened
drew water down, down

in it, with an arm, when the arm
around her neck, Bev's arm would save her.

once there was a canal
as if it was here.

once it drew
drew the world's attention
drew water down. as if.

Bare Creation Myth

They clear away the grass, the trees
Their ploughs open up the ground

In a thousand pairs they tug at roots
Along the low ground.

There is a survey master, an overseer
A foreman

They mark out they plough, they dig
Shallow the pails of food and water they are brought

And unnamed are the women
They press against at night

And now with axes sharp
They set to work upon the western acre

And they plan the course of water
A shallow ditch through frontier lands

Without ancestor in this pungent earth
Though favor toward them is boundless

Glory shall come to this new land

Erie Canal.
There was a sound when spades first hit earth.

Counterweight of Memory
Empire Begins Itself

meanwhile the creak, the churn, the snap
whipsails across an ocean

or silent as a rush of starlings, curiosity noiseless swept
sideways over white-clouded night skies

locust twigs
moth petals

the cyclic
of corn and squash
yellow & loud to the touch

so time's first hour
when was it made no sound

not like hands breaking ground
designed to be quiet like liberty

whose measurements were made in silence
and slowly foot after foot, I think

because someone had to scissor out
the ground, but I only saw a sign that said

it must have been here once

Romeo518:
So he led me to the river with his face

Soul Preacher

I'd squandered sixty-four bones
by the time

he kissed me down
Delaware Avenue

my thumb stalling out in
the nascent
blue of his jeans, a

carnival of beginnings
beating

inside his white shirt
Falling on my knees—

in order to
overtaken

Not Written Elsewhere But between Us

Mostly he
photographs not people
maligned but things, buildings . . .

slumping streets, dotted-line or
dirtied up
unfinished bridges and boats left

roadside. His portraits: tractors
first snow dry dock
one time a scow captain &

often
the
river.

Occasionally us
or my bare
shoulder.
Once, our hands

pinned. Our
meals
belly of an Italian plum I'd bitten in

harvest.
Modest, he pulls toward
rust,

stops fast for tag
sales & anything that looks
abandoned

how we met

Coyote

His outboard motor, fishing poles & cooler
lampshades skewed

pair of jelly jars for drinks (in case), and certainly
two spoons, well, garbage—yes—the freezer

cups with bait six
dozen plastic canisters

of film kept cold
in crisper

black sink, black shower, flaking
stacks of bark in piles

twine & fans of coffee bags
some grounds, book of

trout flies, a knife, some guns
rugless floor, false hinges,

some doors
on or off them

two paper bags
the tomatoes

we picked
bird feeder, wood stove

our muddy boots
upright

by the door
mattress (sweet)

by the fire
on the floor

Tin horns + calico

*Who walked the land
owned the land
leased the land
worked the land
was forced from the land
Who fled & who fought
for the land*

A Cartographer's View in Which Maps Are But Dreams to Nowhere

At first nothing's new: foldout or spiral
maps & GPS have done the work
too familiar

Then drive, let's try the
river, trawl its sides together
then do it all the time

south seeing: means looking for
what's gone neglected
unnamed wordless stuff

Tethered, we are
in a past of blank terrain
so we people it

by imagination
Every dirt road dead end discovery
Each unseen century

Another invisible
Holds us,
mostly

But, to have a present, you have to know which things to forget and which things to remember

So much has leached into this hard land.

One day you took my hand and led me to a place where unromantic things converged: a bridge for trains, iron, a tilted sign for an old canal.

> *Smell of winter*
> > *curiosity pervades*
> *old North River*

We trespassed to the platform, swing bridge, walking the unsturdy wooden planks, standing above the river.

Holding hands, walking closely on the narrow walkway, a wide platform for passing trains beside us. Above the river, wide as it is, the events of invisible centuries hovering. Winter is close & the warmth of discovery is staving off the chill, as the wind is fingering the ends of my scarf.

> *Exposed piers rot*
> > *hidden under high tide*
> *stories unspoken*

Looking out, windswept waters, wondering aloud what once passed up and down, the people who'd made it here, what hills and ridges and forests looked like then, how it was that something called bridges became necessary.

Now the knuckled metal and hinge swing open.

Birdless sky
        1000 adventures, pioneers
facing winter

Your arm about my waist.
Obscure objects of desire.

We are living in the Year 415

So easy to be fooled by 2020
In youth, enduring, this country that contradicts itself with
freedom & many laws & few traditions. commodities, though.
but i know freedom expands beyond the borders of buy and sell.
beyond the borders of truck or car. i know. taproot of capitalism
runs Dutch, runs deep & we are a restless nation and do not say
no. a bargain for a salesmen who waves his dollars nightly. my
home, then, a collection of fragments that survived demolition. our
origins. devoid of context. misunderstood. complexities of injustice
wrapped into simple words (trade). history, kind of a waste, flows
away like the river we live beside. certainly it has a source, is it true
that we lack a story that doesn't involve decimation, exploitation.
a source, flows into the atlantic/blends into the larger attempts to
draw a conclusion. dismissive simplicity prevents me from being
satisfied—a Native a Dutch a smoke stack a dredge spoil a marker
mill circle of fire-cracked rocks small evidence without backstory
so knowing isn't possible, so home: is bigger, but pieces, ruins.
this whole thing's gone subjective and inconclusive and in which
linear relief will come by road, some days I wish I could flee in
all directions at once . . . to the highway, to the highway . . . but
it's all i've got.

787, 90, 87, 20, 5, 9, 9J, 9H, 32, 144

by rail by boat
    as the crow flies, by gull,
by way of Port

River, River

September 11, 1609: & H. Hudson enters a natural harbor
ambitious, he pulls north
magnetic curiosity
marking magnetic declination
Trim the sails
all hands
and head to wind

September 11, 2001: at Albany
damned south they fly, navigating a blue
faith ribbon of river
magnetic anisotropy

Flight 11, craft trimmed, opposes deviations
Angle of tail   angle of incidence   angle of attack
& directionally dependent

Hudson, an easy axis.

cycles of empire
a restless river never still
September morning

Frontier Fortress

places we learned love to
our fingerprints

       all over our loving things
       that every backroad dirt was drove

be no wall, be no floor, be   but home

       so found,
       so touched,

so become my own   familiar

swaddle up mountain
wade down river

buckle together   with six bridge

       yeah, my beyond the borders
       my hundred-mile home

Discovery Glossary of Enchantment

aan de dag

                                      leggen

        ontdekken

                                                    bloot leggen

                    open barren

offen legen

        vinden

                                  tegenkomen

In Which a Dutch Corporation Has This Right of First Discovery:
to get to know or become aware of, usually accidentally, discover or determine the
existence, presence, or fact of; come across, find, meet, learn, discovers, discovering,
discovered

Joseph Henry's Electric Fields
1826

Ascending winter's twinning steps
Academy to school, and two-by-two,
to morning's brick-lined view.

Students, look, he says, *if metals touch*
stable currents charge, let's
bring to life . . . a spark.

He strolls his night,
cobbled home and cold
across a city, ponders dark,

then how magnets wrapped behave,
if iron core   is snugly set . . .
His poverty-clad hands,

once home
toward Henrietta tender—*Darling* (hesitant)
my one request:
Just your wedding dress . . .

Watch closely here: her gown
in strips of silk are torn, bind copper wire
to iron U
to loop to hug to layer, happens—

> *Electric field*
> *to life!*

The Henry. A unit of inductance. Named for Joseph Henry. Albany marks
the birth of a god of the twenty-first century with a tilted blue metal sign in
Academy Park. Where's Academy Park. Electricity. Think about it.

Three Axes of Flight

"In 1910, when the New York World Newspaper offered a $10,000 prize for the first successful flight between Albany and NYC, following the Hudson River, Glenn Curtiss again determined to be first, and did so in a craft he had named the "Hudson Flyer." He won the prize money, nationwide recognition . . ."

Outside the Port
that mysterious fortress of Albany
circles a boy on a bike
with a bag of bottles and cans
texting, what does he know about flight?
Secrets of mastering pitch and roll and yaw.

The rudder's the thing that steadies the yaw.
Glenn Curtiss's sign pitched behind gates at the Port
Hell Rider, he named his plane the Hudson Flyer
our heroes scattered on signs around Albany
the boy sees what we don't because he collects cans
circling with little wings on his bike.

Flying Glenn Curtiss first raced bikes
Frames, tires, body, mastering roll and yaw,
Built motorcycles, then a carburetor with soup cans
Fastest man in the world, but no one goes to the Port.
Our city's history, littered like cans in Albany.
The boy with the empties circling on his street flyer.

Bakken Crude Hustle
2014

All day long
    from North Dakota
        a
            freeform
                fracking
                    congaline
                        of trains
                  veins out
        across the country
transporting
        volatile
           Bakken Crude.
In Albany,
    80,000 barrels
        twice a day
           arrive in
                outdated
           mile-long
      DOT-111s
   sitting
like a string
   of explosive
        black pearls
          on CXS lines
            along 787
                100 paces from the old D&H

stone's throw
from the Hudson
         waiting
              for their cargo
                   to be pumped
                        at the port
                             one car by one car
                                  into storage tanks
                                       then into barges
                             then down the river
                   longshoremen
         working day and night
people in the South End
         bordering the port, wary
    nothing
         can be done
              railroads
                   schedules, contents, commerce
                        regulated
                             by the fed.

Mahican Glossary of Enchantment

PAUPAUTANWUTHYAUK

NGEHCHOIESUMMUK KTOWWOISUMMUK

T'QUAUQUUH

MUMUTTEEHK

MNOTY

MQU(

H-AMUSK

IKUATUAM

WAPEMI

/AUK   SUHKEH

KAU

KAUKSAUKEH

SEPUHQTUHHAUP KENTIKAW

WAUPUNNUHKEUK
CHUCKOPEK

WUH-WEE-MON-OW-KUH-KNAHT   CHEECKKEKANAGH

UHQUAUTOMMAUQUQ
TE'MÓCHAAK

TUSCAMEATICK   HOUSATONIC

---

place of council fire (Albany), ancestors, your animals, autumn, bag of peace, beaver, both sides of the river, chestnut tree, conquer, Coxsackie, NY, crucify, dance, people of the morning (east), Mohicans, white people, this false man, fishing place, forgive us, went home, Greenbush, NY, over the mountain

Anatopophilia: I
Disremembered

A woman tried to live in Albany once though she knew it had become devitalized and the people had forgotten how to hear. She sang little work songs with her hands, moved openly beside the railroad tracks, no one seemed to mind.

She wanted to make sense of the words that remained, reached for those gone missing, lay down some meaning on ones with no pictures (p-a-t-r-o-o-n). Words no one mouths or makes poems about. Words that arrived early. Made empire click, whir. This little machine she lives in. Under the bridge, she traced the sign that said here, and washed by the tide, here, kettle of nations. That said somewhere near here was sacred. She tasted the bitter of what it meant to open up a country by hand. All she wanted was a story just a story so the sleepless man with a shopping cart touched her shoulder, reminded her of this: the tide always rises and weeds will do their work.

map's but one shade of the truth
a flood plain
unwritten, no less alive

acre: a unit of land
(for commerce)
defined

Young Brick Makers in Love

Friday we couple, the tambre, us mixing
unbuckling a week's work not religions, but flexed feet
hooked behind knees

Body beats like heart
"Your face," he whispers "looks like a girl again"

Later in bed,
we talk about brickmaking
the nameless

Let's bring this
place
to life

to 5W

Sunday Septembers us windward, windows down, Rosanne Cash "Motherless Children" from the dash. Route 5 more west, more passing lane than anyone knows what to do with these days. Denim air holds her moonish ring, hovering above us & acres and acres of newly yellowed fields. Night noises noon—the susurrus of insects. Us, me and him, we drive. Out for a look or for a what's left. Much, and also not much. Here's what: River. Town. Smokestack. Statue of Liberty popped on concrete blocks. Shingle shack. Windowless woman walking gaunt. At intervals, signs remind us a canal still locks. And unlocks. Car for sale. Bale of hay. 3(0)(00)(000)(0000) years fret a landscape, here our patinated confluence of defeats. Is it that fewer people people isolation's periphery. Is it that firm resolve of weeds. This terrain, a lance, a breach, a coppered knot between us. Car for sale. Bale of hay.

Mile after mile
roadside totems
littered, lingering, left

Grain
1948

Shoveling
in the Port on Saturdays,

Peter ((twelve children))
for extra money

Margaret ((twelve children))
boiling water for bath night.

I wonder if he rode the bus with
his shovel or walked home carrying it

at midnight.
Did he borrow one?

Rope barge to dock,
((her apron, his swollen feet))

did all the men climb into the hull
or was there a chute?

How many and was it soft beneath
their boots

or feet
where did all the children sleep?

Before bed did he stroke her hair
Did she towel grain dust from his

Albany, NY, a port city for 400 years. Once furs + every kind of pelt, canoes to sloops. Now grain. Now oil. Molasses. Wood. Turbines. In and out of the country. Turkey. China. Jamaica. Work is a private country.

South End, October 2015

I woke up, got dressed,
and went out to look for home again. Walked

down a bike path & noticed bittersweet
working its way through railroad ties

through pallet stacks, on up the felted stems of sumac
Its tangle swaying fiery in the leafless trees

& it screened a parking lot of crushed cars
& the tumbling drums of Clemente cement mixers

Stray tendrils reached for a chain-linked overpass
and red berries were splitting from their brittle yellow jackets

as a few seagulls wheeled above my head
    beneath pigeon-colored skies.
Down below, on 32

I watched a light rain gloss a heavy-duty wrecker,
red, chromed out, safety lights flashing. As it slowly

exited the lot I felt awkward, an intruder
standing there, watching it merge with the stream of men

driving flat beds, dump trucks, hauling scrap & fill
downshifting past housing projects and dull-colored box cars

heading down a dozen unnamed roads
toward the sound of train whistles

& the sound of crawler cranes booming cargo,
toward the grain elevators & oil tanks

that mark mysterious countries of men
working together beneath a city's averted eye

Anatopophilia: II
Loosestrife

there was a woman once she tried to live in albany so she mimicked all the routines but found they had gone dark already. she followed footpaths to jobs and back and woke mechanically on saturday to men energetic with mowers. which meant prayers would be pointless so she drew a black wheel that turned and turned and turned and let no one off until . . . she found it had become her own.

that's it, she said, a city i do not love. then the sign beneath the 7-8-7 bridge nudged her. hey it said, i was once the kettle of native nations. once. and the woman said it's just everything's gone invisible. there are things i want to see. but you . . . ? the sign agreed, closed its eyes for centuries. sparrows fought for crumbs at her feet. but still, the woman believed.

Natural Glossary of Enchantment

        eagle

              herring

          alewife

shad

        channel cat   *cormorant*

          finch   *piping plover*   *redwing*

blackbird   *mink*

     hudson confetti

        mergansers

             striped bass pike   *hudson beef*

otter

   dutchmen's breeches

             stinking benjamin

     loon   *crayfish*

peregrine   *pigeon*

             gull

We're exhausted & excused,
just 400 short years and

our birth rather burly:
So let's be clear;

we know just enough
to sell the Half Moon

back to the Dutch
Those steamships

we invented, the Hudson River Line, good-bye.
We're in good company, though

those chalky letters on bridges
forgetting they spell

New York Central

Dirty Harry's Laundromat
November, 2016

Grinning, I saw what remained of your teeth,
triangles, black, a gap where the front one used to be.

We talked for a few minutes, discovered we both
had dads who'd up and moved to Florida.

Looking for something else, I guess. "The south,"
you said, "is not me. It's the truth.

Everything I know is here on the street. I know my way
around, not like down there." "I know what you mean," I said.

"Look," you said, "all these leaves and paper tore up on the
    sidewalk, I like this."
You told me about your sister, robbed the Mobil station,

the one over there on the corner.
"Heroin. She had a gun, but . . .

She's been face down in concrete for awhile.
I think she's raisin' up now."

I told you my brother had never robbed a Mobil,
but, yeah, he was raisin' himself up, too.

"I sleep back here," you said, pointing, "behind the laundromat
and here people give you things. It's all right. Like

Just last night, this lady come out of Price Chopper, handed me
    this giant
20-pound turkey. I said, *Lady, look,*

I ain't got no where to cook this.
She goes, *Well, then, like, trade it.*

So I did. Got myself fifteen bucks for it."
We laughed

South Pine Sunday
Everyday, 2015–2018

In slow *sohbet* another day with rake
with broom with awkward walker
Mr. B's *goooo maw-niiin* . . .
salutes South Pine Avenue.

His shuffled cadence cottoned
steps the steps, one then one then one
his boxer's ears stone deaf

abruptly falls then rises, his voice
like his right hand draws from
a bag of grass seed,
in his walker's wire basket

and gripping with his left, cool tube
of aluminum, steady, old man, steady, you're
solid as an H

Within the small cage of his
lawn, yard-stained khakis, navy jacket
and thumb-thick spectacles
contender

"From the beginning, the colony existed under the auspices of the Dutch West India Co., whose directors had a narrow vision of it, as a thing to be exploited for profit. The settlers, however, quickly developed different ideas . . ."

A Description of New Netherland (1655)
by Adriaen van der Donck

South Pine Backyard, 2014

& how excruciating
to watch night

come on
the way the mockingbird

spins
through her staggering routine

while a pair of cardinals zip line
between grape vine & cherry tree

the knot
of sparrows riffling in the magnolia foliage.

Along the back fence, a row of
pines blacken as if

Bob Ross has just dropped in
for a visit, fanning and varnishing away at dusk

behind the garage adding three
alpine spears, some happy accidents. The neighbors

tools are still, finally,
and I am sitting

on the stoop while a
plane arcs &

the cat sees a moth
spring up

which she swipes immediately & I watch its
chalky life twitch fiercely

beneath her paw
& realize how quickly
this ends

You Connect Me to Here

Cardona's winter market window, cured meats hanging
warm bread dusted, shelved, and divided by size. With
cheese rounds, a cashier sells olives marinating
like a *mercato centrale*, plates of stacked biscuits
in elegant cellophane pyramids, for Christmas.

On the *Italia*, *mi nonno*, just six years old
docks in Ellis, Pietro holds the little hand of his
brother Pasquale, they're alone in the New World
it's night, Statue of Liberty silhouette faces
them, kids like toys tumbled rough through raven masses.

Nonno, best you farmers forgot Italy—
You told your own kids: *We're American now.* No
mi cara, not *amore*, nor one family recipe
for sauce. I envy Cardona's December window,
and me, a few simple stories. Still, *ti penso*.

---

ti penso (Italian) - *I think of you*

city: I've walked every one of your streets
& raised a child beneath

your copper beeches
& counted them

in times of misery, do I
cling to the walls of your naked cage of place?

the question
heart asks,

holding wrists, curving up throat
across tongue

and out pale
          lips - *city, do I just drive away.*

while
raking every one of my

three-thousand-nine-hundred-and-eleven nights
well then, tether me, city,
and surrender.

Open the door
of all the things I care for

I won't die
waiting

          commerce
                    without creation myths
          Port of Albany

Path to You
Pangburn Road

They go to work.

They take the path 23 Truck Plaza ⇒ Terminal 50 ⇒Boat St. ⇒ Tug St.

I come to you.

I take the path 20W left at Golden Fried ⇒ right on Dunn Memorial ⇑ over old North River ⇒ into Ren-suh-leer (not a native name) ⇒ pass Liquor Shed ⇑ pass waste water treatment smoking fence ⇒ Yankee Doodle ⇒ Signature Auto Ranch ⇒ Hardcore Ink ⇒ beyond Big Lots and every little light on Mary's porcelain head ⇒ to bend at the 1812 Encampment ⇒ to enter the manor & the surface joys. . . . sometimes, I wonder if it's real.

Regardless, the names are ugly.
What matters is the land between us.

When you come to me.

On the Road to Coeymans

1. What We Speed Past
Juan's Crack is OK

Begging, the white man with cardboard sign is asking Rensselaer drivers for burger money, is leaning beneath the bridge. McDonald's has his back. Bus shelter's plastic blues with bicycles, she is painting with polish her pink XXX name away. Pacing, the black man is circling Golden Fried & Mobile Boost & little girl someone's in candy stripes tosses all her napkins white into the air. Little boy someone's chases them toward the road. Paper flags

2. Come to Jesus in the Pastures
Morton & Pearl

She canes across cobblestone the woman toward the cat and the
dollar store toward the pick-up and the sumac so the awkward
method of the boy with the jumprope so the girl with leopard
leggings strides to Platnym Motor Sales so men splaying across
wood stairwells to the way every red light is fizzing the way

J E S U S

A

V

E

S is fizzing above the bus shelter as spring in the streets
is arriving as children into the playground backlined with boxcars
to the shopping carts planted in the DMV parking lot while the
sign *port tavern* is yellowing while most everything is crepitating
to fish to jazz to tibetan flags disarranged put to fluttering from
dan o'connell's cash only cafe.

3. Shorty Deli, Inc.

If you see the pickup with the dashboard skull, you're getting closer. Keep going past condemned red xs and heavy weight DJ downtown beyond intercoastal eighteen-wheeler and there's the tat boy with a fat calf cross delivering Snapple to Shorty Deli, for Historic Cherry Hill homeless manstroller and woman grocery cart. Egg sandwiches over easy for you and you and you. Now run. Completely out of Albany.

4. $3.50 for a dozen farm fresh eggs

Every time I see that sign on your lawn, sir, I break in thirds, split white from black, split work from pity, split freedom from forgiveness and beg myself for beauty. Ask myself if I'm just two hands made of grudge and jury, then I can cut a wedge from this pie of blame knowing my salvage corner is still plain tin. A foot can only tap relief in one direction, that's out of here. Tortured road, 144, tortured every day, sir, you force me to see what I don't want to know. Like why's your old skidoo still parked out by the mailbox, why's there chickens on it? Are you listening? Or are your ears tuned down, boys laughing up in the barge crane cab at jokes I don't even get.

PS: There's a vulture on your RV.

5. Henry Hudson Park

An eagle drawn from deadwood &
transparent river skin
herons drop in graceful pairs
across evening's setting sun.

Eastern shore, your homes are tilted
toward a river never still
on western shore, a sycamore
with cambered arms above

a rotting barge
it's partially submerged
their fists of iron fierce, forgotten
a century's inventions slurred

Oblivious, this boy he's playing
dodging tables on the green
wields his bow across the water
shoots an arrow from its string

6. Greene County is Purple Heart Country
High Tide at Hannacroix, January

Wash up Wednesday: one 25-ounce Natty Daddy, aluminum blue crushed to hell in the crosshatch of driftwood. As civilization discards, river returns: Milk jug. Bobber. Spent shell. Tampon blue applicator frozen, tip-up, in dewclaw. Crescent of beach firmly frozen. Shush of tide sloughs north.

Ice cleaves 2:30. In the reeds, neither duck nor goose. Nothing flies. Nothing breathes. Both tidal pond and tributary. Snake vines in winter's twist, every locust choked. When I stand at the river and look out, it happens like this: My ache. My spreading bruise. My commitment.

> *Solitude*
> > *gunshot backdrop*
> *mute as January*

What's in a name? That depends. Coeymans' residents engaged in a long-standing, turn-of-the-century argument in the town paper over origin & spelling. One: *Honey croy kill.* Another: *Honnicroix,* French colloquialism. This, for its Dutch association: Uncle Peter's barn went adrift during a flood, with a crowing rooster on its uncertain peak. Thus, it is *Hanna croix,* literally "crowing creek." In response: *We do protest against the naming of a truly majestic creek after a common barnyard fowl.* Back atcha: *its derivation trivial but its German origin not to be lightly scouted.* Or: "swift river curly crimped and intricate.." With certainty: Hanacroy, *so let the Indian (swift river) be retained, but only if the spelling is not too involved. . . .*

O frivolous compound.

Whose voice was first heard in this land?
—Spotted Tail to President Hayes

1600

The Flatts are part of the first la
purchased by Kiliaen Van
Rensselaer for his patroonship o
Rensselaerswyck, 1630.

Native Americans trade beaver skins
to the Dutch for European goods.

A hous
Arent V
an impo

points made from traded brass,
A.D. 1700.

Living Glossary of Enchantment

freshwater tidal   marsh

broadleaf   spatterdock

pickerel weed

arrow   leaf

rosette-leaved aquatics

mid plantain

narrowleaf   cattail

river   bulrush

butter weed

wild rice

blue flag

bur-reed   shoal

water hemp

sedges   estuary

joe-pye-weed

sneezeweed

spotted jewel weed

false pimpernel

monkey flowers

yellow iris

bittercress   sand flats dredge spoils

fresh water intertidal mudflat

plants submerged in high tide

Mountains and rivers remain

Let It Be Unnamed
Down by the River, May 2016

Let there be no maps
no trails
take down the sign

let guys in safety orange
have their secrets
their sons in waders, too

let a red bird
hop between white
branches that reach

out over some ruin
or other
let the stories

we unearthed
moss
let high tide

swallow
it
plus our

footprints
all of it

Coxsackie Grasslands
May

box cars slow
        beside a buried thresher

mockingbird
        above butterweed

expansive view
        of Catskills

#pullovernow

New Baltimore
May

another unworded place

        turning toward where the river must be

below, muddy rocky beach
silence

        stone wall crumbles

sea glass
railroad spikes

        brick chips nest in the roots of old trees
        the past asleep in my palm
        motor boats bound up and down

fisherman anchors his pale
        yellow skiff

        cold water,
        broken stone

A Field Outside Athens on a Sunday Night

Cresting a country road, I drive, and a girl appears,
playing with her dog while across the road
two teenage boys in a paddock
—I can hear them laugh as I pass—
fly a kite.

A skinny mutt turns as if on cue,
and races toward home, where a pick up truck
is just pulling into the driveway.

Around the bend, six kids in sweatshirts
are playing volleyball beside a faded red barn
that looks exactly the way you need
a faded red barn to look. Off in the distance,
lambs baah for effect.

Further down the road, the peepers are turned up
to just the right volume, and the air is tangy
with manure. If you long for the Catskills, they're on your right,
navy against a melon sky. On your left, the river valley, a pale mist.

The sun is going down
on a field outside Athens, and just before
the curtain drops, a mockingbird replays her day
once more, just for you,
as you pass out of Athens into night.

Twilight Alley

when green was surrendering to night

buoys were winking private codes in pairs

and tankers were rusting their way south

Beside the river I was watching

ribbons of clouds slide

off the tilted mask of dusk

1

Harriet Cany (Mrs. Rembrandt) Peale, en Plein-Air 1858

Steel cage crinoline discarded
Worn leather boots pecked with wax laces
Skirt carmine, petticoat, trailing moss
Braid loose, stays loose
Robin's egg ribboned & wide-brimmed straw sailor
Rembrandt's wooly vest over - let's face it -
a white blouse that isn't very white.
Riding out and dipped across her cheeks,
no king's commission on her mind.
Only running, climbing, seeing & finding
Brushes, paintbox, her paper,
The way that Hudson River breathes light
this valley. . . . mountains. . . .

Here, Harriet. Chase it. Track it. Memorize its rays and paths. . . .

"A confluence of factors made landscape painting a particularly difficult pursuit for even highly talented nineteenth-century women. The vast majority of formal art academies did not admit women and a prevailing Victorian prudishness did not permit females to draw or paint from nude models. Female artists were often excluded from prestigious art clubs and therefore barred from an important means of cultivating patrons. There was also an overarching social prejudice against women painting outdoors. Many did not deem women physically capable of the rigors of plein-air work. Worthington Whittredge (1820–1910), a highly regarded Hudson River School painter, grumbled that women's dress got "in the way of climbing about rocks and over precipices" and, in addition, "they do not know how to stick an umbrella spike into the ground."

— Antiques and Fine Art

Harriet Cany Peale Succumbs to Light While Regarding the Transcendence of Nature

lemon leaves
tipped

tawny murmur, drawn
silver-shaded boulders

daubed lichen-lit geometries
planed surfaces

I could anchor here in navy crevasses,
stretched limbs bare
reaching

Hudson Valley Light

Route 9
between, beyond the pines

through a break in the pines
farm beyond red, Catskills sloped, sloped around violet

bewitched by, rays, in rays of raking light
sheer goldenvarnish, girds, spreads

pastels profusely surfacing settling
bathing, yellows coruscation every surface

beyond

Good Things at Malden Bridge

wading across
            sunshine
little fishing creek

beneath the bridge we
stripped in a rill

at sunset & in forgiveness
& heat photographed

ourselves ridiculous
so it was after

the laughter after
all, my lips blistered

with the salt
of you, and i did

learn you love
too quickly
to learn

Leçons de Choses

From the French school child's exercise in which an object is described once from a scientific point of view and once from a literary point of view

A. The Water Chestnut

Family: Trapaceae

Trapa natans L.

Origin: Europe, Asia and Africa

Produces a nut-like fruit that can be cooked or eaten raw and has been cultivated in China and India for at least 3,000 years.

Habitat: Lakes, ponds, canals, and slow water.

Distribution: It has been declared a noxious weed, with most problematic populations occurring in the Connecticut River Valley, Lake Champlain region, Hudson River . . .

Threat: Once established, it can reduce oxygen levels.

Infestations can limit boating, fishing, swimming . . . its sharp fruits, if stepped on, can cause painful wounds.

Description: An annual aquatic plant with submerged stem.

The floating leaves are fan-shaped, triangular with toothed edges, 0.75 to 1.5 inches long, forming rosettes which float on the surface. Each leaf has a spongy inflated petiole that enables the rosette to float. The plant produces new leaves from a central terminal meristem in the rosette. The plant's cord-like stems are spongy and buoyant and can reach lengths of up to 16 ft. The stems are anchored to the substrate by a branched system of fine, long, profuse roots.

Eradication is difficult as seeds may lay dormant up to 12 years.

Heavy metals have been found to accumulate in the edible parts.

(See General Electric, see battery manufacturers, see nickel cadmium, see polychlorinated biphenyls.)

B. The Water Chestnut

skipped from ornamental garden to nature, and never turned back.
So ubiquitous floating green herb

You, with scalloped, tender leaves
coverlet, sprouted quilt, sudden blanket

rocking on sunny summer tides, rhythmic cover
nesting in mud flats, clogging intertidal shallows, matting shore

They say you even drown the light—
Fifteen-foot tether root, hairy vein of swaying life

Approach the surface,
whorled rosettes surround, protect

half a dozen patient faces, green, unblinking, biding time,
four-horned baby seed devil

September, Canoeing in at Stockport Creek

When I lie down at night, I am afraid I shall not live till morning, and when I rise up in the morning I am afraid I shall not live till night; I am so harrassed with the War. — River Indian, 1748

Six-Cent Redemption

No shame in working, Violet says
her life, for sale, "best offer" and spread across
the lawn unmowed

Maze-like, mismatched metal
tools and things, weather worn
table tops and broken

The Flats, she says, so poor
those stupid Irish pulled railroad ties
for firewood. Ties, you know, were soaked

In creosote. Squinting toward a heavy
sky, that mess, how hard it was back then
with kids and finding work, a matchstick

Factory, wraps her hair, a plastic bonnet
the shame, she says defiant, as rain begins to fall
is in not working, turns toward her withered home.

Stockport Flats. From a typed, half-piece of paper picked up at a garage sale: *On September 17, 1609, Hudson stopped for a day at the mouth of what is now known as Stockport Creek, territory under the control of the Mohican Indians . . . At one time, this was the hub of industrial activity in Columbia County. Waterpower was abundant and the historical evidence suggests that the motivation behind the Town's formation was to benefit the proprietors of the many woolen mills along these sources of waterpower. . . . The Columbia White Sulfur Springs was located in the Hamlet of Stottville, at the southern end of Town. In the mid-1880s, these sulfur springs were as well known as those of Saratoga. People came from great distances to drink and bathe in the water. The mills and spas are long gone.*

Not Another View of Delft

Emma Willard
A rent war
Mary Powell scrapped

Nutten Hook

A cargo barge sneaks up the way a storm front can, catching us with our backs turned. Even the sound, its low double-hull rumble like thunder . . . Afrodite glides straight toward us through pack ice, four-hundred-and-fifty-feet of jet black bulk, red flag to 'fore, red tug 'round back and white radar bars twirling like batons. Inside the tug, an invisible 500-hundred-ton master of motor vessels gentles her south, piloting 120,000 barrels of oil port to port, estuary to ocean. Afrodite passes so close we step back

> *river reeds bend*
> *in her wake*
> *then bow*

Flood Tide

& a thawing
grey-green
climbs again
above the

berm
and again the Mahican sand fields
at Papscanee flood,
we're leaving

our boots
on the wood bench
& wade in & two
carp are cleaving
now too far inland
to live

Hudson River Morning along 9J

Let's forget the garden
of vermillion poppies,

and great blue herons
with hanging legs

Let's turn away
from the sloping swoop of wild canaries,

and the brown, full-fanned tom
pacing the hillside

No reason you'd notice a crow
strutting across train tracks,

or gaze at lilting gold feathers
of swamp weed, without me

Without you, I won't listen for morning's cool breeze,
hear its leathery patter in aspen leaves.

Let's agree, we'll walk away from the river
close our eyes to the centuries we saw.
We won't speak of ships again,

still time to pretend we saw nothing,
no empty paper cups, neither suns nor moons
blazing toward the shoreline

Pay no mind, either, that miniature kayaker
stroking across the shipping lane,
a piece in a child's playset,

brown hair blowing
her tiny yellow paddle.

Forgetting is Incremental

The first thing to go is the scent
then fades memory of touch
laughter, the last

In sleep
your fingertips on my face
story me awake

I attempt small fires of recollection
they blaze, recede

Sentiment scarlets
before exiting

We know
from experience
longing withdraws

Lucky if our names take up residence
in other mouths

Frozen Glossary of Enchantment

water sky land sky

                    black ice sheer ice   candle ice

        grease ice glazed   bummock

                                    very close pack ice

            frazel ice

                                calving from an ice shelf

        rafted ice

                    sastrugi

                    polyna   finger-rafted ice

        fast ice

                                pancake ice

            ice foot

                    ice blink

                            brash ice

                    growler   plate   drift

floeberg

            pancake   ice field

                            open pack ice   slush

hummocked ice, with coagulated spicules

        then, when tributaries jump their banks

Get the Window on the Right
Memorizing a Landscape/Amtrak at Rensselaer

The two-and-a half hour train ride to Manhattan begins in Rensselaer, with dawn, with concrete and graffiti. Up here, plastic and paper streamers baffle in the weeds. The ground is pale, naked, punched down, with a few rusty rails leading nowhere.

Facing south, we get the window on the right. The whistle blows, our train is off and getting up to speed. Five minutes we're already rushing beside the Hudson River, its tributaries blossoming thick with broom weed, poised, waiting for early sun to glow golden. Pulsing past at 75 miles-per-hour, the pastel blues and pinks of dawn are giving way to morning.

The train whistles again, announces our fast approach to crossings at Papscanee, Hamilton Printing, boat club at Castleton. At a parallel, through the bare trees, silent barges with empty hulls urge north by silent tugs, for oil. Or pushing south, loaded with grain bound for Ecuador. There are kills, duck blinds, and dozens of inlets already beginning to fill with water chestnut.

Across the river, on a narrow island, an eagle's nest, twigs and sticks knit into a huge, rustic bowl, visible for a few seconds. The great blue heron, legs trailing, here then gone. And on the narrow strip of land between tracks and shore, tangled masses of vines cloak spring's early growth. Little flags of green appear, wave, and vanish in a horizontal blur.

Then a tiny, tidy clapboard structure, white, appears and we can see a splash of light in water. I notice it's a foot or two above the high water line. Then, swallowed by woods.

Now the view exhales, slowly fanning out on the Three Sisters. Their violet faces framed by breaking day, their peaks haloed by the dark distant V of flying geese. Before them, the width of the river ripples, sapphired.

What of this lighthouse? These moorings? And here, these pier pilings? Down there an old barge, bare skeleton of rotting wood and spikes. A beaver dam. Remnants, our story. Nearly meaningless signs we don't know how to read.

One hundred years ago, ferries ferried back and forth. For decades, the Mary Powell steamed up and down. Gone though. All of it. Still, I look for clues, thinking it all meant something once, each tide, each discarded object, each ignored gate or inlet or abandoned building. Now, for pleasure, this yacht club, these speed boats docked, fishing boats still covered, and sailboats with bare masts, gently swaying in their slips

Aftersong

3am & I am watching insomnia
pirouette behind my eyes, its thin finger is tapping my forehead
   as I wait
for the narrow tunnel
of light that resembles the approach of day. My skin is busy

performing a crenelation, little trapezoids
of time creasing, dappled with fine hairs, a wrist
& arms preparing to surrender to a tomorrow that won't arrive,
   so I get up, get dressed and before long I'm

walking across Albany, and coming upon a man with a tarp
who is asleep
in among the thin felt of sumac. I am stepping over
him, climbing the stairs of the Livingston Avenue
swing bridge and
recall the wart lady at the grocery store

where I worked when I was sixteen, how she used to come into
   the store
three or four times,

or more on government holidays, her face and neck and hands
   lidded with
fleshy bumps, and she would buy little things: cellophane
   wrapped
packs of Generic 100 Cigarettes, or vegetables trapped in
   styrofoam from the day-old
cart. I wondered if this
was all she did—shop—& I snorted with arrogance. Never
   imagining myself the kind of woman who would be stepping
   over homeless men at night,
looking south, over a crepe-colored Hudson

River, which is rippling so silently away tonight, and while I am
   facing south I am wondering
if this is like the blackness
that surrounded Lincoln's funeral train when it

stopped in Albany, wrapping the dip of oars as he was ferried in
   his long casket across the river
from the east side to the west, coming into the city &
   everywhere draped with crowds, thousands and thousands of
   men & women & children impatient

through the night for the arrival of mortality. I am leaning on
   this rusted rail, holding my shoes
and I am watching nesting geese among the pylons below.

The bridge operator silent in his office, within his square box
on top of the trestled X, his locks
& switches & gears in place, lets me trespass

and while he is opening the tiny blue spigot on his cooler for a
   drink
of water, the sudden

rumble of a diesel engine kicks on in Rensselaer. Passengers are
   riding down the urine-stained escalator to board and take
   their seats inside
a train which smells of industrial disinfectant and not mint or
   melon or butter
and maybe scanning Rensselaer's
weak graffiti for letters that spell their names

& the bridge is humming wood soaked creosote and humming
   iron
and the train whistles as it unhinges itself from the station, and
   now the train is huffling toward me. Time pinned to the slow
clack, rotating, gathering the strength to fully depart, in the way
   I don't seem to be able to fully depart from anything,
and as it passes me there by the guard rail

I notice people with coffee colored
eyes and the hard profile of a man wearing the yellow
shirt of expectation. Across the aisle from him a young couple
from West Virginia is on their honeymoon
to Niagara Falls. His palm rough on her bare leg and I think
   she must be whispering something to him that sounds like
   "there are some things
I would rather not do alone" which I can't help but agree with,
   as she tucks her smile inside the checkered collar
of his shirt & the train vanishes into dawn's waxy din.

A pair of snowy egrets wade along low tide and their bodies
are reminding me of question marks. Then suddenly I am back
   on my street, before the carnival of its soft
survivors emerge, the neighbor's garden hose still coiled

still dripping in the window well, their flag rumpled & caught
   on the eaves, waiting

to be set free, and the cottonwood at the end
of the block must have exploded while I was out. I am climbing
    the stairs
of my apartment, then to my bedroom,

& wondering how many more years I'll be able to get away
    with
traversing a city at night, like the furious child who ran away
    once when she was six &
whose memory is pouring over me then stiffening
into the mask of sleep

Instagram: spetrie_100milehome
A view into some of the details of Albany, Troy, the Hudson River.

Notes

Images, titles, references, further thoughts

P1: photo of Hudson River with barge. P3: Albany, where I live, is said to be the longest continuously settled region of the original thirteen colonies. Pilgrims seeking religious freedom did not arrive in New York and settle here. No. A Dutch corporation settled here. A Dutch corporation that created a system of feudal white indenture. Probably one of the reasons Massachusetts feels different right away when crossing over its border. Regardless of the social issues, the Hudson River, and upstate, have a long and storied history that includes helping open up America. The people who lived upstate did the work to open things up. Many people don't seem to know that history, or care too much about it. But decorators enjoy using bricks and industrial remains in bars while the people who made the bricks and the industrial remains are often invisible. This region was also home to inventors, innovators, and dreamers. They changed the world. We aren't taught their names, or what they did. P4: The  shore of the river is littered with fascinating artifacts, including fish bones. P6, 8, 10: Mount Ida Falls in Troy, which I discovered out walking one winter when I was 9, and still return to. P12: Hudson River morning. It may look ordinary, but thousands of years are right here, in plain sight. You just have to know the language, and know what to look for. P15: Van Rensselaer shipping mark. The van Rensselaer's started a system of white indenture that lasted until the Civil War. And, many things bear their name, too (Rensselaer Polytechnic). We don't seem to know how to invoke their name correctly. P17: Henry Burden (Burden Iron Works) amassed the wealth of a modern-day Bill Gates. The Troy waterwheel was fabled to have been a magnificent working wonder, and to have inspired the ferris wheel. P20: photo of Christmas child. P23: Glossary of enchantment—concept adapted from writer Robert Macfarlane, who suggests we reawaken words that aren't used in order to "re-en-chant" a place, to sing it back to life. P28: Landmark H20vliet: In 2013 St. Patrick's cathedral was demolished. A true landmark patterned on a French basilica. While some of the remains could have been incorporated into the grocery store on its space, they weren't. Its presence has been completely obliterated. They are—at least—good at cleaning up. P30: Abandoned building, Troy, at the confluence of the Hudson and Mohawk Rivers, home of the Industrial Revolution. Quote Elias Khoury interview in *Paris Review*—The Art of Fiction#233. P31: my grandmother swam in the Erie Canal. Of course she did. P34: Hoffman's Playland relocated beside Huck Finn's Furniture Warehouse & More on Erie Boulevard. Erie Blvd. That's where Lock One used to be. Can you imagine opening up the country . . . by hand? Today, there is no hard evidence of that epic location. P36: photo of Hudson River looking north, with the water trail of what I think is a beaver. Beverwijck. Dutch for "beaver district" then later, Albany. A beaver became a monetary standard equal to 8 guilders. They were also extinct before 1700. The difference between a pilgrim seeking religious freedom and a Dutch corporation? Shake your money maker. P38: *Tin Horns and Calico* is the title of the book that describes the rent wars, which involved throwing off (finally) the system of indentured white servitude that characterized much of what is now Rensselaer County and persisted until the Civil War. See van Rensselaer. See Alexander Hamilton. P40: Title drawn from the same *Paris Review* interview with Alias Khoury. P41: We Are Living in the Year 415. New York as a western idea has been around a little over 400 years. Compared to China's calendar, it's not much. There is still a lot to do. P42: Sept 11 is a charged date for New York. Flight 11 pilots followed the Hudson to the World Trade Center. The photo is a screen grab of a painting by Len Tantillo called "Curiosity of the Magua, 1650," where Mohawks approach the ship of a Dutch settler. It's fabled that Henry Hudson entered the mouth of the river on Sept 11. 1609. P43: "Frontier Fortress," also known as "Border Fortress"—names drawn from a genre of Chinese poetry that deals with the experiences—real or imagined—of life on the edge of the Empire. The people (and poetry) of those in the trading borderlands, outside the thriving populated areas, was different. I think of upstate as the edge of Empire. Remote. Subject to extremes. Somewhat hostile. Ha. P44: Sketch Albany from Papscanee. P45: Joseph Henry lived in and taught in Albany, and, along with Michael Faraday, is credited with the discoveries leading to the electrical industry. We have a crooked & inconspicuous blue-and-yellow historic marker tucked away in Academy Park announcing Albany's role in the invention of a god of the twenty-first century. I would think it's worthy of a museum. P46: Glenn Curtiss made the first long-distance flight, down the Hudson from Albany to Manhattan, using technology borrowed (without permission?) from the Wright Brothers. The court systems and patents explains why we know more about the Wright Brothers than Glenn Curtiss. The ambitions of daredevils rarely align with laws. P47: oil of unregulated composition came through Albany for a while, during the fracking boom in the Dakotas. P49: Upstate grey. P53: While it has been said the Mohican were actually chased out of the region by the Mohawk (for purposes of a trade monopoly with Europeans), white settlement has borrowed from native terms, but no one really knows what any of it means. Unusual pronunciation adds another complication. Terms from the online resource *Mohican Dictionary* by Lion G. Miles. P54: A chorographical map of the Province of New-York in North America, divided into counties, manors, patents and townships; exhibiting likewise all the private grants of land made and located in that Province . . . (credit: Library of Congress). Maps break land into saleable packets. But what about maps of imagination? Desire lines? Cut throughs and shortcuts? P57: when you drive the wide open lanes of 5W, you see there's a hell of a lot of pavement and only a few cars. P58: my grandfather shoveled grain in the port for extra money. The port is off the beaten track and because it is hidden, it's easy to forget Albany has a port. P61: "Here and washed by the tide . . ." this sign under the 787 bridge acknowledges Fort Orange and the early meeting of Dutch and Iroquois in the 1600s. Museum anyone? P62: the Hudson River is a tidal estuary and, but is often understood as an object of commerce, a commodity to be managed, a thing to navigate. More than a fisherman's paradise. It also flows through a complex, often breath-

taking world-class landscape and is brimming with natural history and species that have survived, been reintroduced with much care after being hunted or fished to extinction, or are protected. See the Hudson River Almanac. P63: Albany sold the Half Moon back to the Dutch a few years ago. Also, New York Central— the name of the railroad that consolidated the upstate line (see Erastus Corning) and the downstate line (see Vanderbilt). Who knows Erastus Corning, and should he enter the literature of our imagination? P66: fragment of a Dutch document burnt in the 1911 fire at the NYS capitol building. "The fire was catastrophic and it was devastating culturally, but they began the rebuilding phase immediately and did a tremendous job," said Jim Jamieson, Capitol architect. "There's really no remaining evidence of the fire." *Times Union*, 2011. P70: I wish I knew more of my family's Italian heritage. P71: I was tethered to the region for 18 years while I raised my daughter. P73: detail from an iron park bench. P75: Dan O'Connell was the wing man to Erastus Corning II, who was mayor of Albany for 42 years. Everyone seems pretty ok with that. The corruption here is legendary, and often people laugh and joke about it. Albany is a one-party town. P77: The river is magnificent. P81: A timeline located at Schuyler Flatts, where the van Rensselaer's had a farm. A building from the grounds was sold and transported to Williams College, then eventually burned or something. P83: Mountains and rivers last. People come and go. P89: Harriet Cany Peale is a largely unknown but talented Hudson River School painter. Olana, near Hudson, is the home of famed HRS painter Frederic Church. There has been a fantastic exhibit of just the HRS women painters. P93: the water chestnut chokes up Hudson river inlets. P97: Emma Willard was the first woman to set up a school to educate women in a manner similar to men. (Troy, NY) The Mary Powell was the name of the "Queen of the Hudson," a well known and beloved side-paddle steam ship built in 1861 that ran on the Hudson for over fifty years. In 1920, it was (you guessed it) sold for scrap. . . . Photo of the seal on Albany's city charter (1686). P101: sketch of the ice factory along 9J. P103: Driftwood holding a brick. You never know what you'll find down by the river. P105: Natural beauty in the region abounds. P108: Hudson Valley landscape. P109: riverboats hauling. P104: cast image of Mary Powell beneath an overpass in Albany. P114: Shells like open hands. We try, we give our best. Hopefully, something beautiful remains.

PS: Don't forget the bricks.

A three-hundred-and-fifty year industry along the Hudson gone invisible except for a couple of ghosty kiln sheds near Kingston. And the occasional scatter of red chips you can find along the banks of the river.

Acknowledgments

Thank you, Sofia, for cutting me a wide swath for all my disappearing acts. And for providing a reason to return to the Capital District nearly two decades ago. Thank you, James, for boosting my photos and believing there was something worthwhile here. Thank you, Brooke, for encouraging me again and again and again to stick with it. Thank you, Tina, for believing in my creativity. Luz and Jaime, for not minding my long periods of absence and for your continued interest and friendship. JW and LW, thanks for the memories and laughter and heartbreak and insight along the way. JE, I wish you were still alive to see this. Thanks for not listening when I said no. Mark, thanks for seeing into my creativity and for your invaluable role in helping guide this project to fruition. Lisa, thanks for your creative patience. Diane, I appreciate your kind humor. Sue, how nice to see you here and I'm so glad for your expertise! And finally, to Bennington College for providing the directive: "Read 100 books, write one."

Author photo by Peter Lawrence.